# SCHOLASTIC

# READING

## SATs TESTS

# YEAR 3

**SCHOLASTIC**

Scholastic Education, an imprint of Scholastic Ltd
Book End, Range Road, Witney, Oxfordshire, OX29 0YD
Registered office: Westfield Road, Southam,
Warwickshire CV47 0RA

www.scholastic.co.uk

© 2019 Scholastic Ltd

123456789  9012345678

A British Library Cataloguing-in-Publication Data
A catalogue record for this book is available from the British
Library.

ISBN 978-1407-18304-6

Printed and bound by Ashford Colour Press

**Author**
Catherine Casey

**Series consultants**
Lesley and Graham Fletcher

**Editorial team**
Rachel Morgan, Tracey Cowell, Anna Hall,
Sally Rigg, Shelley Welsh and Rebecca Rothwell

**Design team**
Nicolle Thomas and Oxford Designers and Illustrators

**Cover illustrations**
Istock/calvindexter and Tomek.gr / Shutterstock/Visual Generation

**Acknowledgements**
Extracts from Department for Education website © Crown Copyright. Reproduced under the terms of the Open Government Licence
(OGL). www.nationalarchives.gov.uk/doc/open-government-licence/version/3/

The publishers gratefully acknowledge permission to reproduce the following copyright material: Catherine Casey for the use of
'Dinosaurs', 'A letter from Adam', 'The Dinner Queue' and 'Odysseus and the Cyclops', 'Ancient Greece', 'The Willow Pattern plate', 'Solar
Eclipse', 'Sports day', 'Strawberries', 'King Henry VIII and his many wives' and 'The tortoise and the hare'. Text © 2015, Catherine Casey.
Every effort has been made to trace copyright holders for the works reproduced in this publication, and the publishers apologise for
any inadvertent omissions.

Illustrations: Moreno Chiacchiera, Beehive Illustration
Photographs:
Test A: © Marcio Jose Bastos Silva/Shutterstock; © Metha1819/Shutterstock; © 3Dalia/Shutterstock;
    © Fresnel/Shutterstock; © Catmando/Shutterstock; © Bob Orsillo/Shutterstock; © Monkey Business Images/Shutterstock.
Test B: © Debra James/Shutterstock; © Padmayogini/Shutterstock; © Igor Zh./Shutterstock; © Timmary/shutterstock.
Test C: © minicase/Shutterstock; © Stephen Dukelow/Shutterstock; © Tim UR/Shutterstock; © Stuart Ford/Shutterstock;
    © Steve Lovegrove/Shutterstock; © MaraZe/Shutterstock; © Georgios Kollidas/Shutterstock; © Everett Historical/Shutterstock;
    © photos; © Everett Historical/Shutterstock; © nicoolay /istock; © Georgios Kollidas/Shutterstock.

# Contents
# Reading: Year 3

| Contents | Page |
|---|---|
| **Introduction** | |
| About this book | 4 |
| Advice for parents and carers | 5 |
| Advice for children | 6 |
| Test coverage | 6 |
| **Tests** | |
| Test A | 7 |
| Test B | 28 |
| Test C | 49 |
| **Marks & guidance** | |
| Marking and assessing the papers | 69 |
| Mark scheme for Test A | 70 |
| Mark scheme for Test B | 73 |
| Mark scheme for Test C | 76 |

# About this book

This book provides you with practice papers to help support children with end-of-year tests and to assess which skills need further development.

## Using the practice papers

The practice papers in this book can be used as you would any other practice materials. The children will need to be familiar with specific test-focused skills, such as reading carefully, leaving questions until the end if they seem too difficult, working at a suitable pace and checking through their work.

If you choose to use the papers for looking at content rather than practising tests, do be aware of the time factor. The tests require a lot of work to be done in 1 hour as they are testing the degree of competence children have – it is not enough to be able to answer questions correctly but slowly.

## About the tests

Each Reading test consists of texts covering different genres and contains 50 marks. Each test lasts for 1 hour, including reading time.

- Reading texts: children may underline, highlight or make notes.
- Questions: children should refer back to the reading texts for their answers.

The marks available for each question are shown in the test paper next to each question and are also shown next to each answer in the mark scheme. Incorrect answers do not get a mark and no half marks should be given.

There are three different types of answer.

- **Selected answers**: children may be required to choose an option from a list; draw lines to match answers; or tick a correct answer. Usually 1 mark will be awarded.
- **Short answers**: children will need to write a phrase or use information from the text. Usually 1–2 marks will be awarded.
- **Several line answers**: children will need to write a sentence or two. Usually 1–2 marks will be awarded.
- **Longer answers**: children will usually need to write more than one sentence using information from the text. Up to 3 marks will be awarded.

# Advice for parents and carers

## How this book will help

This book will support your child to get ready for the school-based end-of-year tests in Reading. It provides valuable practice and help on the responses and content expected of Year 3 children aged 7–8 years.

In the weeks leading up to the school tests, your child may be given plenty of practice, revision and tips to give them the best possible chance to demonstrate their knowledge and understanding. It is important to try to practise outside of school, and many children benefit from extra input. This book will help your child prepare and build their confidence and ability to work to a time limit. Practice is vital and every opportunity helps, so don't star too late.

In this book you will find three Reading tests. The layout and format of each test closely matches those used in the National Tests, so your child will become familiar with what to expect and get used to the style of the tests. There is a comprehensive answer section and guidance about how to mark the questions.

## Tips

- Make sure that you allow your child to take the test in a quiet environment where they are not likely to be interrupted or distracted.

- Make sure your child has a flat surface to work on, with plenty of space to spread out and good light.

- Emphasise the importance of reading and re-reading a question and to underline or circle any important information.

- These tests are similar to the ones your child will take in May in Year 6 and they therefore give you a good idea of strengths and areas for development. So, when you have found areas that require some more practice, it is useful to go over these again and practise similar types of question with your child.

- Go through the tests again together, identify any gaps in learning and address any misconceptions or areas of misunderstanding. If you are unsure of anything yourself, then make an appointment to see your child's teacher who will be able to help and advise further.

## Advice for children

### What to do before the test

- Revise and practise on a regular basis.
- Spend some time each week practising.
- Focus on the areas you are least confident in to get better.
- Get a good night's sleep and eat a healthy breakfast.
- Be on time for school.
- Make sure you have all the things you need.
- Avoid stressful situations before a test.

### What to do in the test

- The test is 60 minutes long. You should allow time to read the texts and then answer the questions.
- Read one text and then answer the questions about that text before moving on to read the next text.
- You may highlight, underline or make notes on the texts.
- There are 50 marks. The marks for each question are shown in the margin on the right of each page.
- Make sure you read the instructions carefully. There are different types of answer.
  - Short answers: have a short line or box. This shows that you need only write a word or a few words in your answer.
  - Several line answers: have a few lines. This gives you space to write more words or a sentence or two.
  - Longer answers: have lots of lines. This shows that a longer, more detailed answer is needed. You can write in full sentences if you want to.
  - Selected answers: for these questions, you do not need to write anything at all and you should tick, draw lines to, or put a ring around your answer. Read the instructions carefully so that you know how to answer the question.

### Test coverage

Children will need to be able to:

- Give and explain the meanings of words
- Find and copy key details.
- Summarise main ideas from more than one paragraph.
- Use details from the texts to explain their thoughts about them.
- Predict what might happen.
- Identify and explain how information is organised.
- Show how writers use language to create an effect.

# Test A

# Dinosaurs

## Introduction

Dinosaurs lived on the planet millions and millions of years ago, before they mysteriously died out. There are several theories as to why dinosaurs became extinct but no one really knows.

Scientists learn about dinosaurs by studying their fossils and bones. Scientists who study dinosaur fossils are called palaeontologists. Many dinosaur fossils are still being discovered today.

There are hundreds of different types of dinosaur. Scientists put them into groups depending on what they ate, how long ago they lived and their body shape.

Learning about dinosaurs and how they lived is fascinating. Read on to find out about some of the most well-known dinosaurs, which are often used in films and cartoons.

## Some well-known dinosaurs

### T-rex

Tyrannosaurus rex (T-rex) was a ferocious, meat-eating dinosaur. It had large, pointy teeth to crush through bones as it ate other animals and dinosaurs. It would walk around on its two powerful legs and had two small arms. T-rex was an enormous dinosaur.

### Triceratops

Triceratops walked on four legs and had a huge head. It had three horns on its head, which is why it is called Triceratops. The word *triceratops* means three-horned head. Many scientists believe the horns were used for protection from the meat-eating dinosaurs.

The horns were up to one metre long. Triceratops also had a large neck collar, which protected it from other dinosaurs. Triceratops would have grown up to nine metres long and been very heavy. Surprisingly, it ate plants and flowers. Triceratops is believed to have been a lonely dinosaur as its bones are usually found on their own and not in groups.

### Stegosaurus

Stegosaurus is often remembered because of the triangular, bony spikes all along its back. It walked on four legs and had a noticeably tiny head! Stegosaurus was lighter than Triceratops. Its front legs were a lot shorter than its straighter back legs. Stegosaurus ate plants and flowers. It is believed that Stegosaurus would have lived within a family or group.

### Diplodocus

Another plant-eating dinosaur, Diplodocus would have eaten leaves from high up in trees and on the ground. Diplodocus is recognisable because of its extremely long tail and neck. It walked or plodded around on four legs of equal size. This long dinosaur most likely lived within a family or group.

### Brachiosaurus

This dinosaur is well known due to the large nostrils at the top of its head. Brachiosaurus had a long neck that stretched upwards so it could reach leaves and plants high up. Its tail, however, was fairly short. Although Brachiosaurus would have walked on all four legs, its front legs were much longer than its back legs.

**Which is your favourite dinosaur?**

# A letter from Adam

Apple Tree School
Apple Tree Road
London
AB1 2CD
info@appletree.sch

23 January 2016

The Dazzling Dinosaur Museum
Dinosaur Road
London
DD1 2MU

Dear Mrs Green,

I am writing to say thank you for showing us around the Dazzling Dinosaur Museum. My school friends and I all agreed it was definitely dazzling! I had an amazing day looking around the museum and learning all about the dinosaurs on our school trip. The information boards were very colourful and easy to read. The talk you gave was really interesting and funny. Thank you for answering all our difficult questions. It must be great working at the museum.

However, I was disappointed that we had to spend *so* long waiting to get into the room where the Tyrannosaurus rex skeleton was. Even though we had tickets we still had to queue for hours and hours. It was so boring waiting and my feet began to ache just standing there. I think it was really unfair that we wasted so much time queuing when we had bought tickets. As a school group we should be able to go straight in.

My favourite part of the day was watching the dinosaur film about the Tyrannosaurus rex and it was so funny when some of my friends screamed. I couldn't believe how big all the dinosaur skeletons were and that we were allowed to hold a *real* dinosaur bone!

Many thanks again for showing us around. I hope you are able to sort out the queuing problem.

Yours sincerely,
Adam

PS Perhaps you could give us free tickets to visit again to say sorry for having to queue. (Just an idea.)

# The Dinner Queue

My tummy began to rumble,
My tummy began to talk,
I was feeling so hungry,
I didn't mean to grumble.

My tummy began to bubble,
My tummy began to gurgle,
I was feeling so hungry,
I was hoping to have double.

The dinner queue was so long,
The dinner queue went on and on,
The other children laughed and talked,
My tummy began its own song.

My tummy began to groan,
My tummy got louder and louder,
The dinner hall was noisy but,
My tummy; it let out an enormous moan,

The dinner hall fell silent.

My face began to go red,
My face began to burn,
Everyone found it funny,
I think perhaps tomorrow I will have a packed lunch instead!

# Odysseus and the Cyclops

The tale of Odysseus and the Cyclops is an ancient Greek myth.

The waves crashed against the side of the small, fragile, wooden boat. The men aboard were tired and hungry. They had been travelling over dangerous waters for weeks with no sight of dry land. Suddenly, Odysseus, who was the leader, spotted a small island. Feeling hopeful that they would find food and fresh drinking water, the men stepped onto the island. At first this felt very strange after being on the rocking boat for so long, and some of the men fell over. In the distance they could hear sheep so they set off to investigate.

Slowly, the men walked across the wet, yellow sand until they found a large cave. The tired men thought the cave would make an excellent shelter while they slept. When they entered the cave they were amazed to find huge baskets full of food and the biggest bottles of water they had ever seen. They couldn't believe their luck!

Odysseus suggested that they should wait until the owner returned to ask him if they could have some of the food and water but the men were so hungry they couldn't wait. They stuffed themselves with the unusual fruits and plants that filled the baskets. They ate all the bread even though it tasted soggy and lumpy. Finally, the men drank the water from the bottles to wash down all the food they had eaten. After their feast, the men rested on the large straw bed that was big enough for them all.

The men were woken up by a thumping sound that shook the ground. Something enormous was approaching the cave! The steps got louder and louder as they got closer and closer. Suddenly, one of the large bottles smashed on the floor as the ground shook with each thump. The *thing* was getting closer. While the other men hid in the corner of the dark, damp cave, Odysseus stood fearless, ready to confront the approaching creature.

An enormous shadow fell over the entrance to the cave. The men hiding at the back trembled with fear. Odysseus stood tall with his shield held in one hand and a weapon in the other. The owner of the cave appeared. A huge, ugly creature filled the whole entrance with his muscly body. A few strands of red hair poked out from the top of his head. Sweat dripped down his pink cheeks. Under each arm the creature held three lambs and behind him was a whole flock of sheep. He wore old sandals on his large, smelly feet. One of his toes,

which was almost as big as Odysseus himself, looked mouldy and sore. It had yellow pus oozing out under the toe nail. A large single eye that filled most of the creature's face stared into the cave. It was a Cyclops! And he was angry.

The sheep suddenly flooded the cave and surrounded Odysseus and his men. Then the Cyclops rolled a large boulder over the entrance to the cave. It was completely dark and the men were trapped. They could feel the fluffy sheep around them. Over the noise of the sheep Odysseus told the men not to worry because he had a plan.

In the morning, the Cyclops rolled the boulder out of the way to let his sheep out. Bright sunshine flooded the cave. Quickly, Odysseus threw his sharp spear at the Cyclops and hit him in the middle of his one eye. The men ran out of the cave and towards the shore. The blinded Cyclops stormed after them but the men were already pushing their small wooden boat out to sea. The angry Cyclops threw heavy, round stones at Odysseus and his men, and let out an almighty roar that echoed over the waves as the men continued their journey.

## Test A

**Questions** 1–13 are about *Dinosaurs* on pages **8–9**.

Marks

**1.** When does the text say dinosaurs lived on the planet?

Tick **one**.

fifty years ago ☐

hundreds of years ago ☐

thousands of years ago ☐

millions of years ago ☐

1

**2.** How do scientists learn about dinosaurs?

_____

1

**3.** Name one way scientists group dinosaurs.

_____

1

**4. Find** and **copy** the sentence in the *Introduction* that tells you the author finds learning about dinosaurs really interesting.

_____

_____

1

Marks

**5.**

> *...they **mysteriously** died out.*

What does the word *mysteriously* mean?

Tick **one**.

without an explanation ☐

very slowly ☐

really obviously ☐

very quickly ☐

1

**6.** The author has chosen the phrase *crush through bones* when describing T-rex's teeth. What effect does this language have on the reader?

Tick **one**.

The word *crush* makes it sound like the dinosaur is in love. ☐

The word *crush* shows how powerful the dinosaur's teeth were and how they destroyed the bones. ☐

The word *crush* makes it sound like the dinosaur liked hugging violently. ☐

The word *crush* is soft and gentle. ☐

1

**7.**

> *T-rex was an **enormous** dinosaur.*

What does the word *enormous* mean?

_____

1

**8.** Name **three** different dinosaurs mentioned in the text.

1. _____

2. _____

3. _____

Marks

◯

1

**9.** In the text, which dinosaur ate meat?

_____

_____

◯

1

**10.** Name **two** dinosaurs that ate plants and flowers.

1. _____

2. _____

◯

1

**11.** Which features of the Diplodocus make it easy to recognise?

_____

◯

1

SCHOLASTIC National Curriculum SATs Test

**12.** Draw lines to match the dinosaur to the correct description.

Marks

| T-rex |
| Brachiosaurus |
| Triceratops |

| large nostrils at the top of its head |
| a large neck collar |
| a ferocious, meat-eating dinosaur |

1

**13.** Which dinosaur had three horns on its head?

_____

1

Marks

---

**Questions** 14–21 are about *A letter from Adam* on page **10**.

**14.** What greeting does Adam use in the letter?

Tick **one**.

Mrs Green, ☐

Hello Mrs Green, ☐

Dear Mrs Green, ☐

Hi there Mrs Green, ☐

1

---

**15.** Where had Adam been on his school trip?

_____

_____

1

---

**16.**

> ...it was definitely **dazzling**!

What effect does the word *dazzling* have on the reader?

Tick **one**.

It makes the museum sound boring. ☐

It makes the museum sound old. ☐

It makes the museum sound blindingly bright. ☐

It makes the museum sound amazing and special. ☐

1

---

**17.** What was Adam's favourite part of the day?

_____

_____

Marks

1

**18.** Give **two** reasons that Adam enjoyed the school trip.

1. _____

2. _____

2

**19.** Why didn't Adam like queueing? Give **two** reasons.

1. _____

2. _____

2

**20.** What did Adam think of the dinosaur museum?

Choose **two** points he makes in the letter and write them below.

1._____

_____

2._____

_____

2

**21.** Give **two** pieces of evidence that show that Adam would like to visit the museum again.

1._____

2._____

2

Marks

**Questions** 22–27 are about *The Dinner Queue* on page 11.

**22.** In the poem, what is the character waiting for?

_____

_____

1

**23.** Which word in the text rhymes with *moan*?

Tick **one**.

home ☐

phone ☐

groan ☐

bone ☐

1

**24.** Why was the character's tummy making lots of noises in the poem?

Tick **one**.

He was poorly. ☐

He was hungry. ☐

He was bored. ☐

He was naughty. ☐

1

**25.**

> *The dinner hall fell silent.*

What effect does this line have on the poem?

_____

_____

1

**26.** Why did the character in the poem go bright red?

**Tick one.**

He was embarrassed. ☐

He was cold. ☐

He was holding his breath. ☐

He was happy. ☐

1

**27.**

> *I think perhaps tomorrow I will have a packed lunch instead!*

Give **two** reasons why the character in the poem may have said this.

1. _____

2. _____

2

Marks

**Questions** 28–40 are about *Odysseus and the Cyclops* on pages **12–13**.

**28.** Why did Odysseus and his men stop at the island?

Give **two** reasons.

1._____

2._____

_____

2

**29.** When the men arrived on the island, why did some of them fall over?

_____

_____

_____

2

**30.** Why did the men first go into the cave?

_____

1

**31.**

> *...they were **amazed** to find huge baskets full of food...*

What does the word *amazed* mean in this sentence?

Tick **one**.

surprised ☐

scared ☐

hungry ☐

unhappy ☐

**Marks**

1

**32.** What did the bread that the men found in the cave taste like?

_____

_____

1

**33.** Why does the author describe the Cyclops as *huge and ugly?*

Tick **one**.

To make the Cyclops sound friendly. ☐

To make the Cyclops sound scary. ☐

To make the Cyclops sound happy. ☐

To make the Cyclops sound mysterious. ☐

1

**34.** Which **two** words does the author use to describe the Cyclops's feet?

1. _____

2. _____

Marks

1

**35.**

> *Something **enormous** was approaching the cave.*

Write a word you could use instead of *enormous* without changing the meaning.

Something _____ was approaching the cave.

1

**36.** **a.** How were the men in the cave feeling as the Cyclops approached?

The men were feeling _____

**b.** What evidence is there in the text?

The evidence in the text is _____

_____

1

1

**37.** How did the Cyclops trap the men in the cave?

_____

1

**38.** Why do you think the Cyclops was angry? Give **three** reasons.

1. _____

2. _____

3. _____

Marks

**3**

**39.**

> ...sheep suddenly **flooded** the cave...

What does the word *flooded* mean in this sentence?

Tick **one**.

It shows that the sheep were drowning in the water. ☐

It shows that the sheep rushed in like gushing water. ☐

It shows that the cave flooded with water. ☐

It shows that the sheep couldn't swim. ☐

**1**

**40.** What do you think would have happened if they had waited before eating the food, like Odysseus suggested?

_____

**1**

**End of paper**

# Test A Marks

| Question | Focus | Possible marks | Actual marks |
|---|---|---|---|
| 1 | Information/key details | 1 | |
| 2 | Information/key details | 1 | |
| 3 | Information/key details | 1 | |
| 4 | Making inferences | 1 | |
| 5 | Meanings of words | 1 | |
| 6 | Explaining/identifying choice of words and phrases | 1 | |
| 7 | Meanings of words | 1 | |
| 8 | Information/key details | 1 | |
| 9 | Information/key details | 1 | |
| 10 | Information/key details | 1 | |
| 11 | Information/key details | 1 | |
| 12 | Summarise | 1 | |
| 13 | Information/key details | 1 | |
| 14 | Information/key details | 1 | |
| 15 | Meanings of words | 1 | |
| 16 | Information/key details | 1 | |
| 17 | Information/key details | 1 | |
| 18 | Making inferences | 2 | |
| 19 | Information/key details | 2 | |
| 20 | Information/key details | 2 | |
| 21 | Making inferences | 2 | |
| 22 | Making inferences | 1 | |
| 23 | Explaining/identifying choice of words and phrases | 1 | |
| 24 | Making inferences | 1 | |
| 25 | Identifying/explaining how information is related. | 1 | |
| 26 | Making inferences | 1 | |
| 27 | Making inferences | 2 | |
| 28 | Information/key details | 2 | |
| 29 | Making inferences | 2 | |
| 30 | Information/key details | 1 | |
| 31 | Meanings of words | 1 | |
| 32 | Information/key details | 1 | |
| 33 | Meanings of words | 1 | |
| 34 | Explaining/identifying choice of words and phrases | 1 | |
| 35 | Meanings of words | 1 | |
| 36 | Making inferences | 2 | |
| 37 | Information/key details | 1 | |
| 38 | Making inferences | 3 | |
| 39 | Meanings of words | 1 | |
| 40 | Predicting | 1 | |
| | Total | 50 | |

# Test B

# Ancient Greece

Ancient Greece refers to a time in history over 3000 years ago. During this time, the Greek people had lots of new ideas about how to live that inspired others around the world. They invented the Olympic Games and had radical thoughts about science, including medicine. They enjoyed and developed the arts and also tried out the idea of governments ruling, where ordinary people could have a say instead of being ruled by one powerful person such as a king.

Zeus God of the Sky whose symbol was the thunderbolt

## Greek gods and goddesses

The ancient Greeks believed in lots of different gods and goddesses who controlled the world around them on a day-to-day basis. The ancient Greeks believed that they had to please the gods and goddesses and keep them happy, otherwise they would punish them. There was a god or goddess to represent each different area of everyday living such as the home, love, beauty, music, war, rain and even the sea. Each one had a special symbol and power. For example, Zeus was god of the sky and his symbol was the thunderbolt. The gods and goddesses had qualities similar to humans but were extremely powerful and immortal. The ancient Greeks built temples for them which were very decorative and had large columns that held up the roof. They would pray and leave gifts for the gods and goddesses at the temples.

## Pottery

Ancient Greek pottery is well known and easily recognisable. The ancient Greeks made bowls, cups and jugs from clay. The clay was a red-brown colour when it dried, and was decorated with black pictures of everyday life. It is these decorations that historians have used to understand what life during ancient Greek times was like.

### The Olympic Games

The Olympic Games began in ancient Greece, although the modern Olympic Games are very different! During ancient Greek times, the games were held in Olympia every four years. Events such as running, wrestling, discus throwing and chariot racing took place. Women were not allowed to take part. Apparently, the men didn't wear any clothes while competing! The winners received olive wreaths to wear on their heads.

### Clothes

Ancient Greek women wore tunics made from large pieces of cloth. The tunics went all the way to the ground and had a belt around the waist. They usually wore their long hair tied up in beautiful hairstyles with headbands. The men also wore tunics but they were usually knee-length. Sometimes they would wear sandals, but often they had bare feet.

### Athens and Sparta

Ancient Greece was divided into different cities. Each city had its own rules and way of life. Athens and Sparta were two of the most important cities. Evidence suggests that life in these two cities would have been very different. Spartans did a lot of physical exercise and had a large army, whereas Athenians spent more time learning and enjoying the arts.

# The Willow Pattern plate

It was Sunday afternoon and I was visiting my Great Aunty Alice. I loved it at Great Aunty Alice's house; it was so warm and wonderfully welcoming. Each room was full of interesting objects Great Aunty Alice had collected from her travels, such as African drums, clogs from the Netherlands, Moroccan silks, an Australian didgeridoo and beautiful Indian jewellery. Great Aunty Alice had been to so many wonderful places when she was younger.

She had such fascinating stories to tell. Great Aunty Alice had made a huge, sticky chocolate cake, which we enjoyed with cups of freshly brewed tea. I noticed the teapot, cups, saucers and the plates all had an interesting blue and white pattern on them. After I had finished eating the cake, there under the crumbs I saw a picture. My delicious cake had been hiding a picture. In the middle of the plate was a Chinese building surrounded by a beautiful garden and a high fence. There was a bridge with three characters running over it and two doves in the sky. Great Aunty Alice saw me looking at the plate as she sipped tea from her china cup. "Beautiful plates, aren't they? They are from England but reminded me so much of my trip to China I had to buy she told me her version of the love story on the famous Willow Pattern plates...

There once lived a very wealthy man who had a pretty daughter. (I imagined this to be Great Aunty Alice when she was younger but of course it wasn't really.) The wealthy man had chosen a husband for his daughter but she had fallen in love with a servant who worked at their house. The man was very angry as he did not feel the servant would make a suitable husband for his precious daughter. In anger he banished the servant from the house and built a high fence around the gardens, keeping his daughter safely inside.

The daughter was very unhappy and spent her days walking up and down the fence inside the garden which contained a willow tree. Then one day her father announced there was to be a party and she would meet her future husband. The daughter was even more upset. However, the very clever servant crept into the house among the many hundreds of guests and together they ran away. The wealthy man spotted the couple running over the bridge and chased after them but they managed to escape.

Afterwards the couple went to live on a faraway island and for many years they were very happy together. The servant became a famous writer, but the wealthy father heard about this and tracked them down. The servant was captured and killed. The beautiful daughter soon died of a broken heart. The two doves on the plate symbolise their everlasting love for one another.

As she finished the story a single tear appeared in Great Aunty Alice's eye and I knew she was thinking of someone she had once loved and lost.

# Solar Eclipse

Suddenly it went dark,
Hundreds had gathered at the park,
In the middle of the day,
The sun had gone away.

People had come out to see,
How could this possibly be?
The sun was covered by the moon,
I hoped it would be back soon.

What a wonderful amazing sight,
But you mustn't look *directly* at the light,
Special safety glasses are a must,
To protect your eyes, in this you must trust.

It only lasted for a while,
The safety glasses were ruining my style,
The moon quickly passed by,
The people gathered let out a sigh.

The sun was back in the sky,
The crowds all said goodbye,
What a magical sight it had been,
A solar eclipse we had all seen.

# Sports day

Jessica stared at the ground as she walked around the edge of the school field. Tears dropped off the end of her nose and plopped onto the green grass. It was lunchtime and all the other children were playing football or chatting excitedly at the other side of the field but Jessica wanted to be alone.

It was sports day and the events started after lunch. Jessica's teacher had put her name down to do the 200m hurdles. But Jessica hated sports day! She was just no good at it and she was worried everyone would laugh at her. She imagined coming last or falling over all the hurdles. It would be so embarrassing.

Suddenly, the bell rang and everyone started lining up on the playground. Jessica spotted her best friend, Amira, coming towards her. Her face went even redder. Quickly, Jessica tried to wipe her tears away so Amira wouldn't see. But Amira did see. She saw Jessica's red, puffy face (at least it would match her team top) and realised how upset she was. They walked towards the playground to line up so they didn't get into trouble. Jessica tried to tell Amira the problem but she was so upset it was difficult to talk. Amira put her arm around Jessica and told her it would be OK.

In the changing rooms, Amira told Jessica that her friends and family all liked her for who she was and it didn't matter if she wasn't great at hurdles as long as she tried her best. Then she listed all the things Jessica was good at, such as drawing, painting and maths. With a cheeky grin on her face, Amira added, "And what you are really best at is taking forever to get changed!" That made Jessica laugh and she felt much better.

By the time they went back out onto the school field, sports day was about to start. There was a carnival atmosphere with music and bunting. The colours of the three school teams shone out around the running track. Families and friends were gathered to watch and cheer on the athletes. Jessica watched nervously as her team-mates leapt and cheered around her. The loudspeaker announced each race and there was a huge board with the results on. Stickers and rosettes were being handed out. Everyone seemed to be having a great time, except Jessica.

Finally, the loudspeaker announced the last race; the 200m hurdles was about to start. Jessica's tummy was full of butterflies as she stood on the start line. The hurdles looked so horrifyingly high. Amira smiled encouragingly at her and mouthed, "You can do it!" across the crowd. The whistle went and Jessica ran as fast as she could. With the wind in her face she flew over each hurdle. Her feet pounded over the hard, sun-baked ground of the running track. Jessica could hear her team cheering and the finish line was in sight. Before she knew it, the race she had been dreading was over. Jessica smiled to herself; she had done it! And she wasn't even last! Jessica had come third, winning an essential point for her team.

Once the points were all counted up, the winning team was finally announced. The crowd cheered and clapped. The red team celebrated loudly by singing and dancing; they had won by one point!

Marks

**Questions 1–11** are about *Ancient Greece* on pages **29–30**.

**1.**

> *During this time, the Greek people had lots of new ideas about how to live that **inspired** others around the world.*

What does the word *inspired* mean in this sentence?

Tick **one**.

scared ☐

influenced ☐

controlled ☐

bored ☐

1

**2.** Who was the god of the sky and had a thunderbolt as his symbol?

_____

1

**3.** What did the ancient Greeks leave at the temples?

_____

_____

Marks

1

**4.** What material did the ancient Greeks use to make cups, bowls and jugs?

_____

_____

1

**5.** What did the pictures show on ancient Greek pottery?

_____

_____

1

**6.** In ancient Greece, where were the Olympic Games held?

_____

_____

1

**7.** Who were not allowed to take part in the ancient Greek Olympic Games?

_____

1

**8.** What did the winners of the ancient Greek Olympic Games receive?

_____

_____

Marks

1

**9.** What were women's tunics made from?

_____

_____

1

**10.**

> Sometimes they would wear sandals, but often they had **bare** feet.

What does the word _bare_ mean in this sentence?

Tick **one**.

a type of animal ☐

uncovered ☐

woolly shoes ☐

cut-down ☐

1

**11.** What have historians used to learn about life in ancient Greece?

_____

1

Marks

> **Questions** 12–22 are about *The Willow Pattern plate* on pages **31–32**.

**12.** On what day of the week does the character visit Great Aunty Alice?

_____

_____

1

**13.** Which adjectives does the author use to describe Great Aunty Alice's house?

Tick **two**.

wonderful ☐

welcoming ☐

inviting ☐

friendly ☐

warm ☐

1

**14.**

> *Each room was full of interesting **objects**.*

What does the word *objects* mean in this sentence?

Tick **one**.

targets ☐

items ☐

houses ☐

people ☐

1

**15.**

*She had such **fascinating** stories to tell...*

What does the word *fascinating* mean?

**Tick one.**

famous ☐

imagination ☐

interesting ☐

boring ☐

**16.** What type of cake had Great Aunty Alice made?

_____

**17.** What colours are Great Aunty Alice's plates?

_____

**18.** Who did the daughter in the love story fall in love with?

_____

Marks

1

1

1

1

**19.** Why did the wealthy man build a fence around the garden?

_____

_____

Marks

1

**20.** Number the events below to show the order in which they happen in the love story. The first one has been done for you.

| | |
|---|---|
| He banished the servant from the house. | |
| The wealthy man spotted the couple running over the bridge. | |
| The wealthy man had chosen a husband for his daughter. | I |
| The beautiful daughter soon died of a broken heart. | |
| The daughter walked up and down the fence. | |

1

**SCHOLASTIC** National Curriculum SATs Tests

**21.** Give **two** reasons why the character in the story liked visiting Great Aunty Alice.

1. _____

2. _____

**22. a.** List **three** places that Great Aunty Alice has visited.

1. _____

2. _____

3. _____

**b.** Explain how you know she has visited these places.

_____

_____

_____

Marks

2

2

2

**Questions** 23–29 are about *Solar Eclipse* on page **33**.

**23.** In the poem, what is a solar eclipse?

_____

_____

_____

1

**24.** In *Solar Eclipse*, which word rhymes with *dark*?

Tick **one**.

spark ☐

day ☐

eclipse ☐

park ☐

1

**25.** Why are the people gathered in the park?

_____

1

**26.** Why do you need to wear special glasses to look at the eclipse?

_____

_____

Marks

1

**27.** Give **one** reason from the text that shows why the writer thinks wearing safety glasses is a good idea and **one** reason why it isn't.

Good idea: _____

Bad idea: _____

2

**28.** In the poem, how does the moon pass by?

Tick **one**.

carefully ☐

quickly ☐

directly ☐

slowly ☐

1

**29.** How does the beginning of the poem relate to the end? Give **two** examples.

1. _____

2. _____

2

Marks

| Questions 30–40 are about *Sports day* on page **34**. |

**30.** Where is the story set?

Tick **one**.

On the school field. ☐

In the park. ☐

In a classroom. ☐

In a sports centre. ☐

1

**31.** At what time of day was sports day taking place?

_____

1

**32.** Which race was Jessica competing in?

_____

1

**33.** Which colour team is Jessica in?

_____

1

**34.** Why is Jessica so upset about taking part in sports day? Use evidence from the text to explain your answer.

_____

_____

1

**35.**

> Jessica spotted her best friend, Amira, coming towards her. Her face went even redder. Quickly, Jessica tried to wipe her tears away so Amira wouldn't see.

How was Jessica feeling at this point in the text? Use evidence from the text to explain your answer.

_____

_____

2

**36.** Find **three** examples in the text that show Amira is a good friend.

1._____

2._____

3._____

3

**37.**

> *Jessica's tummy was full of butterflies...*

What does this phrase mean?

Tick **one**.

It shows that Jessica was poorly. ☐

It shows that Jessica was feeling nervous. ☐

It shows that Jessica was hungry. ☐

It shows that Jessica was feeling cross. ☐

1

**38.**

> *The hurdles looked so **horrifyingly** high.*

What is the effect of the word *horrifyingly* in this sentence?

Tick **one**.

It shows how nobody wanted to take part in the hurdles race. ☐

It shows that the hurdles weren't very high. ☐

It shows how frightened Jessica felt about the hurdles race. ☐

It shows that hurdles should be banned from sports day. ☐

1

**39.** Number the events below to show the order in which they happen in the story. The first one has been done for you.

| | |
|---|---|
| Amira told Jessica that her friends and family all liked her for who she was. | |
| The red team celebrated loudly by singing and dancing. | |
| Suddenly, the bell rang and everyone started lining up on the playground. | |
| Jessica ran as fast as she could. | |
| Jessica was crying at lunchtime. | I |

1

**40.** How does Jessica feel after the race? Use evidence from the text to explain your answer.

_____

_____

2

**End of paper**

# Test B Marks

| Question | Focus | Possible marks | Actual marks |
|---|---|---|---|
| 1 | Meanings of words | 1 | |
| 2 | Information/key details | 1 | |
| 3 | Information/key details | 1 | |
| 4 | Information/key details | 1 | |
| 5 | Information/key details | 1 | |
| 6 | Information/key details | 1 | |
| 7 | Information/key details | 1 | |
| 8 | Information/key details | 1 | |
| 9 | Information/key details | 1 | |
| 10 | Meaning of words | 1 | |
| 11 | Information/key details | 1 | |
| 12 | Information/key details | 1 | |
| 13 | Identifying/explaining choice of words and phrases | 1 | |
| 14 | Meanings of words | 1 | |
| 15 | Meanings of words | 1 | |
| 16 | Information/key details | 1 | |
| 17 | Information/key details | 1 | |
| 18 | Information/key details | 1 | |
| 19 | Making inferences | 1 | |
| 20 | Summarise | 1 | |
| 21 | Information/key details | 2 | |
| 22 | Making inferences | 4 | |
| 23 | Making inferences | 1 | |
| 24 | Identifying/explaining choice of words and phrases | 1 | |
| 25 | Information/key details | 1 | |
| 26 | Making inferences | 1 | |
| 27 | Identifying/explaining how information is related | 2 | |
| 28 | Information/key details | 1 | |
| 29 | Identifying/explaining how information is related | 2 | |
| 30 | Information/key details | 1 | |
| 31 | Information/key details | 1 | |
| 32 | Information/key details | 1 | |
| 33 | Making inferences | 1 | |
| 34 | Making inferences | 1 | |
| 35 | Making inferences | 2 | |
| 36 | Making inferences | 3 | |
| 37 | Identifying/explaining how information is related | 1 | |
| 38 | Meanings of words | 1 | |
| 39 | Summarise | 1 | |
| 40 | Making inferences | 2 | |
| | **Total** | **50** | |

# Test C

# Strawberries

Home-grown strawberries straight from the garden are amazing. They taste sweet and delicious. Ripe, red strawberries are wonderful on their own, with a little cream or in delightful desserts. Think how delicious strawberry tart, strawberries with fresh scones or homemade strawberry ice-cream

are. Strawberries are a wonderful treat. Not only that, they are easy to grow too.

Strawberries can be grown in the ground, in hanging baskets or in pots on the patio, so don't worry if you only have a small garden.

**Helpful hint**

Place a net with small holes over the plants to stop wildlife eating those delicious strawberries before you do!

## Instructions for planting

### Things you will need

- Good-quality strawberry plants
- Moist soil or compost
- Water
- A garden trowel

**Top tip**

*Always* water the soil not the plant! If the leaves, flowers or fruit get wet they could cause the plant to go mouldy.

1. First, choose a spot in your garden or patio that gets plenty of sunlight.
2. Then, make sure the soil or compost is prepared well by watering it and weeding thoroughly.
3. Next, using a small garden trowel, dig a hole for each plant 30cm apart in rows.
4. Carefully, place each young strawberry plant into the hole, making sure you don't damage the delicate roots.
5. Gently, replace the soil around the roots and press it down.
6. Water the soil well.

**Plant** strawberry plants from April to June.

**Harvest** strawberries from June to August.

### Make your own lovely lollipop label

All you need is a lollipop stick and some permanent marker pens. Using the marker pens, draw a picture of a strawberry at one end of the lollipop stick. Then stick it into the ground or soil next to your strawberry plants.

### Secret of successful strawberries

Once the plants have flowered, put strawberry mats or straw around the base of the plant. This stops the fruit from touching the moist soil and rotting before it ripens.

## Recipe for strawberry cheesecake

Once your mouth-watering strawberries are ripe, try making our lovely strawberry and white chocolate cheesecake. Amaze all your friends with this powerful pudding.

## Ingredients

- 400g strawberries
- 200g biscuits or cookies crushed up
- 75g unsalted butter
- 300g melted white chocolate buttons
- 250g tub of cream cheese
- 150g whipped cream

You will also need a greased cake tin.

1. First, grease a 20cm cake tin with a small amount of the butter.
2. Next, melt the rest of the butter in a saucepan.
3. Add the crushed biscuits to the butter and remove from the heat.
4. Quickly, press the crushed biscuit mixture into the base of the greased cake tin and place in the fridge for 30 minutes.
5. Meanwhile, remove the green stalks from the strawberries, then wash the strawberries in a sieve. Chop into quarters.
6. In a large bowl, whisk the cream cheese and whipped cream together.
7. Pour the melted white chocolate buttons into the cream mixture.
8. Carefully, fold the strawberries into the cream mixture, making sure you don't mash the strawberries.
9. Finally, pour the cream, chocolate and strawberry mixture onto the top of the biscuit base and return to the fridge for 2 hours before serving.

### Top tip

To remove the pudding from the cake tin, run a warm knife around the inside edge of the tin.

Enter our 'Best strawberry crop' competition!

Win a trip to the garden show of the year!

For full details check out our website.

*Enjoy summer strawberries!*

# King Henry VIII and his many wives

Henry VIII was king of England for 38 years in the 16th century. In his youth he enjoyed horse riding, hunting and other sports. Henry enjoyed eating and often had grand dinner parties. He had fiery red hair. In his later years, he became very round and had a bad leg that caused him pain. He was a very famous king and founded the Church of England.

Henry had six wives! This poem is used to remember what happened to each of Henry's wives:

*Divorced, beheaded, died.*
*Divorced, beheaded, survived!*

## His wives

### Catherine of Aragon: divorced

Catherine of Aragon originally married Henry's older brother Arthur. After Arthur died, Henry and Catherine were married. They had a baby girl called Mary. Henry was desperate to have a son to become heir to the throne. He decided that Catherine was too old to have any more children. Therefore, he asked the pope to divorce them so he would be able to marry someone else. However, the pope refused as this was against the rules of the Roman Catholic Church. So Henry ordered the archbishop to arrange the divorce. Catherine of Aragon and King Henry VIII were *divorced*.

**SCHOLASTIC** National Curriculum SATs Test

### Anne Boleyn: beheaded

Henry's next wife was Anne Boleyn, a young woman he had fallen in love with. They had a baby girl called Elizabeth. Henry still wanted a son to become king after him. Anne Boleyn was accused of breaking the law and her head was chopped off as punishment. Anne Boleyn was *beheaded*.

### Jane Seymour: died

Jane Seymour was Henry's third wife. They were only married a short time before Jane gave birth to a boy. Henry finally had his son, a baby boy they named Edward. However, Jane Seymour died shortly after the child's birth. She had a queen's funeral. Jane Seymour *died*.

### Anne of Cleves: divorced

It was arranged for Henry to marry Anne of Cleves. However, straight away it became clear that Henry and Anne were not a good match. Henry thought she was ugly and she didn't enjoy music and reading like Henry. They were *divorced*.

### Catherine Howard: beheaded

King Henry VIII thought Catherine Howard was very beautiful and she became Henry's fifth wife. Henry was now ageing, overweight and had a bad leg. The young and pretty Catherine Howard was accused of not being a good wife and her head was chopped off. Catherine Howard was *beheaded*.

### Katherine Parr: survived

Katherine Parr became Henry's sixth and final wife. Katherine looked after the ill king and was a good stepmother to his children. Henry died while they were still married. Katherine Parr *survived*.

### Divorced, beheaded, died. Divorced, beheaded, survived!

# The tortoise and the hare

On the edge of the meadow, which was full of beautiful wild flowers, lived an old, wise tortoise. Tortoise had lived in his wonderful house by the meadow for many years. He was a quiet and polite character who liked living on his own. He spent most of his time lying in the warm sunshine, which made his hard, protective shell even stronger. Every day, after hours of sunbathing, Tortoise would poke his wrinkly little head out of his shell to munch happily on some lovely lettuces. Then each afternoon he would stretch his strong legs by taking a short walk around the meadow, one step at a time, and stopping to talk to his friends on the way. First he would pass friendly Frog sitting by the stream that trickled over the stones. Then there was Worm, who wriggled in the soil, and Honey Bee, who was always buzzing in and out of the colourful flowers. Tortoise enjoyed living by the meadow, until one day a new neighbour moved in.

His new neighbour, Hare, was loud and rude! He bounced around squashing all the flowers and crunched noisily on carrots. He splashed up and down in the stream. Hare played loud, modern music and sang noisily all day. He thumped his huge paws up and down on the ground. Tortoise and the other animals didn't like this at all. Worm found all the noise vibrated down through the soil and made all his tunnels move. Frog found all the horrid cold water splashed over him while he sat relaxing on a lily pad. Honey Bee found the flowers were all flattened and she couldn't make any honey. Tortoise found it very noisy, and his friends were upset.

The animals called a meeting. It was held at Tortoise's house. They decided this simply would not do and Hare must be stopped! After many hours of whispering, discussing and thinking, a plan was finally created.

Politely, Tortoise knocked on Hare's door with the other animals all waiting behind him. A few minutes passed before the door suddenly flew open and out popped a very energetic, bouncy hare. Hare leapt from one foot to the other and was dressed in the very latest running kit.

"Out of my way. Can't stop now. I am going for a run," shouted Hare as he ran past them all. The animals were shocked and angry.

The next day they tried again. Tortoise knocked firmly on Hare's door with the other animals all waiting behind him. Once again the door suddenly flew open and again the young energetic hare bounced out of the door and past them all.

On the third day the animals posted a letter through the door. They waited outside to see what would happen. Honey Bee looked worried, Frog was bubbling with anger and Worm held his breath. Tortoise didn't move as the door once again flew open. This time Hare stood in the doorway with the letter in his hand.

"Since you are all so unhappy with me living here the only answer is either I move out or you all do," stated the hare. "I propose a competition!" he continued. "Whoever is the fastest animal around the meadow gets to stay. Who will race me around the meadow?"

"I will," replied the wise, old tortoise. Frog couldn't believe his ears. Honey Bee fainted. Worm let out a gasp!

The day of the race arrived. The animals gathered nervously at the start line to support their friend, Tortoise. Although Frog had already packed his suitcase, Tortoise was quietly confident. He knew he had experience on his side. Hare was also feeling confident and bounced around smiling to himself. The whistle went. Hare and Tortoise set off around the meadow. Quickly, the young hare disappeared out of sight. Tortoise slowly plodded along, lifting up one leg at a time and placing it in front of the other.

Halfway around the meadow, Hare spotted a massive oak tree. Looking behind him he laughed to himself. There was no sign of the silly old tortoise who was so slow. Hare decided to take a rest in the shade of the oak tree. It was a hot day and he soon fell asleep.

Several hours passed. Tortoise continued to plod around the meadow in the hot sun until he finally crossed the finish line. Loud cheers from the other animals woke Hare suddenly from his sleep. As he rubbed his eyes, he saw Tortoise slowly step over the finish line but he was too far behind to do anything about it.

Slow and steady had won the race!

## Test C

**Questions** 1–15 are about *Strawberries* on pages **50–51**.

**1.**

> *Home-grown strawberries straight from the garden are* ***amazing****.*

What does the word *amazing* mean in this sentence?

Tick **one**.

excellent ☐

shocking ☐

disgusting ☐

terrible ☐

1

**2.**

> *They taste **sweet** and delicious.*

What does the word *sweet* mean in this sentence?

Tick **one**.

adorable ☐

sugary ☐

sour ☐

bitter ☐

1

**3.** What does the text suggest to put over the strawberry plants to stop wildlife eating them?

_____

1

**4.** What **three** things do you need to plant strawberry plants?

Tick **three**.

seeds ☐

water ☐

a garden shed ☐

a garden trowel ☐

a step ladder ☐

moist soil or compost ☐

Marks

1

**5.**

> *Carefully, place each young strawberry plant into the hole, making sure you don't damage the delicate roots.*

Give **two** reasons why you need to be careful when placing the strawberry plants into the holes? Use the text as evidence.

_____

_____

2

**6.** How far apart should you plant strawberry plants?

_____

1

**Marks**

**7.** When can you harvest strawberries? Complete this sentence with the correct months.

You can harvest strawberries from _____

to _____.

1

**8.** Why is it a good idea to put straw or strawberry mats around the base of the plant?

_____

_____

1

**9.** What does the recipe explain how to make?

**Tick one.**

strawberry ice cream ☐

strawberry cheesecake ☐

strawberry tart ☐

strawberries with scones ☐

1

**10.** How much whipped cream do you need in the recipe?

_____

1

**Marks**

**11.**

> *You will need a **greased** cake tin.*

What does the word *greased* mean in this sentence?

_____

_____

1

**12.** How long does the dessert need to be left in the fridge before serving?

_____

_____

1

**13.** Where can you find full details of the 'Best strawberry crop' competition?

_____

_____

1

**14.** Why are the 'Top tips' inside star shapes?

Tick **one**.

They are about stars. ☐

To fill the page with colourful boxes. ☐

To make them stand out so that the reader notices them. ☐

The author made a mistake. ☐

1

**15.** **a.** Where does the text suggest you can grow strawberry plants?

Tick **two**.

a greenhouse ☐

a hanging basket ☐

in a cupboard ☐

a pot on the patio ☐

in the fridge ☐

on a window sill ☐

1

**b.** Why does the text say not to worry if you have a small garden?

_____

_____

1

Marks

| | Marks |
|---|---|

**Questions** 16–28 are about *King Henry VIII and his many wives* on pages **52–53**.

**16.** How long was Henry VIII king of England for?

_____

_____

1

**17.** Which **two** words does the author use to describe Henry VIII's hair?

1. _____

2. _____

2

**18.**

> *Divorced, beheaded, died.*
> *Divorced, beheaded, **survived**.*

What does the word *survived* mean in this rhyme?

**Tick one.**

remained alive ☐

became ill but recovered ☐

was in hospital ☐

was poorly ☐

1

**19.** How many wives did Henry VIII have?

_____

1

**20.** Circle the **two** words in this poem that rhyme.

Divorced, beheaded, died.

Divorced, beheaded, survived!

1

**21.** What was Henry VIII's brother called?

_____

1

**22.** Why did the pope refuse to divorce Catherine and Henry?

_____

_____

_____

1

**23.** Why did Henry marry Anne Boleyn?

_____

_____

1

**24.** What were Henry's **two** daughters called?

1. _____

2. _____

_____

2

**25.** What was Henry's son called?

_____

1

**26.** Why did Henry want a son?

_____

_____

**27.** Which of Henry VIII's wives had their heads chopped off?

**Tick two.**

Catherine of Aragon ☐

Anne Boleyn ☐

Jane Seymour ☐

Anne of Cleves ☐

Catherine Howard ☐

Katherine Parr ☐

**28.** Give **two** pieces of evidence from the text to show why Henry was unhappy with his marriage to Anne of Cleves.

1. _____

2. _____

Marks

1

1

2

**Marks**

> **Questions** 29–40 are about *The tortoise and the hare* on pages **54–55**.

**29.** Where is this story set?

Tick **one**.

a forest ☐

a meadow ☐

a beach ☐

a garden ☐

1

---

**30.** Draw lines to match the description to the correct animal.

| Description | | Animal |
|---|---|---|
| friendly | | Tortoise |
| old and wise | | Frog |
| loud and rude | | Hare |

1

**SCHOLASTIC** National Curriculum SATs Tests

**31.** Why didn't Honey Bee like the new neighbour?

_____

_____

Marks

1

**32.** Why did the animals have a meeting?

Tick **one**.

To organise a party for Hare and Tortoise. ☐

To discuss what to do about Tortoise. ☐

To organise a holiday. ☐

To discuss what to do about their new neighbour. ☐

1

**33.** Why do you think Hare suggested the race?

_____

1

**34.**

> Hare **spotted** a massive oak tree.

What does the word _spotted_ mean in this sentence?

_____

1

**35.**

> *Tortoise continued to **plod** around the meadow...*

What effect does the word *plod* have on the phrase above?

Tick **one**.

It sounds slow and heavy. ☐

It sounds bouncy and light. ☐

It sounds fast and happy. ☐

It sounds quick and fun. ☐

**Marks**

1

**36.** Number the events below to show the order in which they happen in the story. The first one has been done for you.

| | |
|---|---|
| Hare saw Tortoise slowly step over the finish line. | |
| The day of the race arrived. | |
| One day a new neighbour moved in. | I |
| The animals called a meeting. | |
| Hare fell asleep under an oak tree. | |

1

**37.** How did Frog feel about Hare moving into the meadow? Use evidence from the text to explain your answer.

_____

_____

_____

_____

**38.** Why had Frog packed his suitcase?

_____

_____

**39.** How do you think Hare was feeling when he saw Tortoise crossing the finishing line? Explain why.

I think Hare felt _____ because

_____

_____.

**40.** Using evidence from the text, what do you think Hare did after the race?

_____

_____

**End of test**

Marks

3

2

2

2

# Test C Marks

| Question | Focus | Possible marks | Actual marks |
|:---:|:---:|:---:|:---:|
| 1 | Meanings of words | 1 | |
| 2 | Meanings of words | 1 | |
| 3 | Information/key details | 1 | |
| 4 | Information/key details | 1 | |
| 5 | Making inferences | 2 | |
| 6 | Information/key details | 1 | |
| 7 | Information/key details | 1 | |
| 8 | Information/key details | 1 | |
| 9 | Information/key details | 1 | |
| 10 | Information/key details | 1 | |
| 11 | Meanings of words | 1 | |
| 12 | Information/key details | 1 | |
| 13 | Information/key details | 1 | |
| 14 | Identifying/explaining how information is related | 1 | |
| 15 | Information/key details | 2 | |
| 16 | Information/key details | 1 | |
| 17 | Identifying/explaining choices of words and phrases | 2 | |
| 18 | Meanings of words | 1 | |
| 19 | Information/key details | 1 | |
| 20 | Identifying/explaining choices of words and phrases | 1 | |
| 21 | Information/key details | 1 | |
| 22 | Information/key details | 1 | |
| 23 | Information/key details | 1 | |
| 24 | Information/key details | 2 | |
| 25 | Information/key details | 1 | |
| 26 | Information/key details | 1 | |
| 27 | Information/key details | 1 | |
| 28 | Making inferences | 2 | |
| 29 | Summarise | 1 | |
| 30 | Identifying/explaining how information is related | 1 | |
| 31 | Information/key details | 1 | |
| 32 | Making inferences | 1 | |
| 33 | Making inferences | 1 | |
| 34 | Meanings of words | 1 | |
| 35 | Identifying/explaining how information is related | 1 | |
| 36 | Summarise | 1 | |
| 37 | Making inferences | 3 | |
| 38 | Making inferences | 2 | |
| 39 | Making inferences | 2 | |
| 40 | Predicting | 2 | |
| | **Total** | **50** | |

SCHOLASTIC National Curriculum SATs Tests

# Marking and assessing the papers

The mark schemes provide detailed examples of correct answers (although other variations/phrasings are often acceptable) and an explanation about what the answer should contain to be awarded a mark or marks.

Although the mark scheme sometimes contains alternative suggestions for correct answers, some children may find other ways of expressing a correct answer. When marking these tests, exercise judgement when assessing the accuracy or relevance of an answer and give credit for correct responses.

## Marks table

At the end of each test there is a table for you to insert the number of marks achieved for each question. This will enable you to see which areas each child needs to practise further.

## National standard in Reading

The mark that each child gets in the test paper will be known as the 'raw score' (for example, '37' in 37/50). The raw score will be converted to a scaled score and children achieving a scaled score of 100 or more will achieve the national standard in that subject. These 'scaled scores' enable results to be reported consistently year-on-year.

The guidance in the table below shows the marks that children need to achieve to reach the national standard. This should be treated as a guide only, as the number of marks may vary. You can also find up-to-date information about scaled scores on our website: www.scholastic.co.uk/nationaltests

| Marks achieved | Standard |
| --- | --- |
| 0–27 | Has not met the national standard in Reading for Year 3 |
| 28–50 | Has met the national standard in Reading for Year 3 |

# Mark scheme for Test A (pages 7–27)

| Q | Answers | Marks |
|---|---------|-------|
| 1 | **Award 1 mark** for: millions of years ago | 1 |
| 2 | **Award 1 mark** for an answer that says they study dinosaur fossils and bones. | 1 |
| 3 | **Award 1 mark** for any one of the following:<br>● body shape<br>● how long ago they lived<br>● what they eat. | 1 |
| 4 | **Award 1 mark** for: Learning about dinosaurs and how they lived is fascinating. | 1 |
| 5 | **Award 1 mark** for: without an explanation | 1 |
| 6 | **Award 1 mark** for: The word *crush* shows how powerful the dinosaur's teeth were and how they destroyed the bones. | 1 |
| 7 | **Award 1 mark** for any word that means *enormous*, such as big, huge, gigantic, large. | 1 |
| 8 | **Award 1 mark** for any three of the following:<br>● Tyrannosaurus rex or T-rex<br>● Triceratops<br>● Stegosaurus<br>● Diplodocus<br>● Brachiosaurus. | 1 |
| 9 | **Award 1 mark** for Tyrannosaurus rex or T-rex. | 1 |
| 10 | **Award 1 mark** for Triceratops and Stegosaurus. | 1 |
| 11 | **Award 1 mark** for its long neck and tail. | 1 |
| 12 | **Award 1 mark** for all lines drawn correctly.<br><br>T-rex → a ferocious meat-eating dinosaur<br>Brachiosaurus → large nostrils at the top of its head<br>Triceratops → a large neck collar | 1 |
| 13 | **Award 1 mark** for Triceratops. | 1 |
| 14 | **Award 1 mark** for: Dear Mrs Green, | 1 |
| 15 | **Award 1 mark** for The Dazzling Dinosaur Museum or museum. | 1 |
| 16 | **Award 1 mark** for: It makes the museum sound amazing and special. | 1 |
| 17 | **Award 1 mark** for watching the film. | 1 |

| Q | Answers | Marks |
|---|---------|-------|
| 18 | **Award 2 marks** for any two reasons based on the text, such as:<br>• He says he had an amazing day in the letter.<br>• He states that the talk was interesting and funny.<br>• He implies he wants to go back to the museum.<br>• He enjoyed holding the dinosaur bones and seeing the T-rex.<br><br>**Award 1 mark** for one reason given. | 2 |
| 19 | **Award 2 marks** for any two of the following:<br>• It was boring.<br>• His feet hurt.<br>• It wasted time.<br>• They had already bought tickets.<br>• They were a school group.<br><br>**Award 1 mark** for one of the above. | 2 |
| 20 | **Award 2 marks** for any two of the following:<br>• It was dazzling.<br>• The information boards were colourful and easy to read.<br>• He had an amazing time.<br>• He didn't like queueing.<br>• The talks were funny and interesting.<br>• He couldn't believe how big all of the dinosaur skeletons were.<br>• He couldn't believe that they were allowed to hold a real dinosaur bone.<br><br>**Award 1 mark** for one of the above. | 2 |
| 21 | **Award 2 marks** for both of the following as evidence:<br>• Adam enjoyed his day.<br>• He asks for free tickets to go back.<br><br>**Award 1 mark** for one of the above. | 2 |
| 22 | **Award 1 mark** for lunch/dinner/food/meal. | 1 |
| 23 | **Award 1 mark** for: groan | 1 |
| 24 | **Award 1 mark** for: He was hungry. | 1 |
| 25 | **Award 1 mark** for answers that suggest one of the following:<br>• It emphasises the silence.<br>• As a line on its own it creates a pause.<br>• It quickly ends the build-up of the noise. | 1 |
| 26 | **Award 1 mark** for: He was embarrassed. | 1 |
| 27 | **Award 2 marks** for two reasons such as:<br>• So he wouldn't have to queue.<br>• Because he was so hungry.<br>• So he would not be embarrassed again.<br><br>**Award 1 mark** for one reason. | 2 |

| Q | Answers | Marks |
|---|---------|-------|
| 28 | **Award 2 marks** for any answer that suggests two of the following points.<br>• They were tired.<br>• They had been travelling for weeks/a long time.<br>• They were hungry/they were looking for food and drink.<br>**Award 1 mark** for one of the above. | 2 |
| 29 | **Award 2 marks** for explaining that some men fell over because the boat had been moving and the land was stable.<br>**Award 1 mark** for identifying that the men felt strange after being on the boat for so long. | 2 |
| 30 | **Award 1 mark** for shelter/to sleep. | 1 |
| 31 | **Award 1 mark** for: surprised | 1 |
| 32 | **Award 1 mark** for any answer that implies the bread was not very nice, such as:<br>• soggy<br>• lumpy<br>• horrid<br>• disgusting. | 1 |
| 33 | **Award 1 mark** for: To make the Cyclops sound scary. | 1 |
| 34 | **Award 1 mark** for 'large' and 'smelly' (exact words must be used). | 1 |
| 35 | **Award 1 mark** for any word that means *enormous* and makes sense in this sentence, such as: huge, gigantic, massive, giant, immense, large. | 1 |
| 36 | **a. Award 1 mark** for understanding the men were frightened/scared/worried/afraid, or any other word meaning frightened. | 1 |
|    | **b. Award 1 mark** for evidence in the text:<br>They were hiding and/or trembling with fear. | 1 |
| 37 | **Award 1 mark** for he rolled a large boulder/stone over the entrance/doorway. | 1 |
| 38 | **Award 3 marks** for any three of the following:<br>• The men were in his cave.<br>• The men hadn't asked to go in his cave.<br>• The men had eaten his food.<br>• The men had drunk all his drink.<br>• The men were sleeping in his bed.<br>**Award 2 marks** for any two of the above.<br>**Award 1 mark** for any one of the above. | 3 |
| 39 | **Award 1 mark** for: It shows that the sheep rushed in like gushing water. | 1 |
| 40 | **Award 1 mark** for any plausible reason relating to the text, for example:<br>• They would still have got locked in the cave.<br>• They wouldn't have got locked in the cave.<br>• The cyclops would have killed them. | 1 |

# Mark scheme for Test B (pages 28–48)

| Q | Answers | Marks |
|---|---------|-------|
| 1 | **Award 1 mark** for: influenced | 1 |
| 2 | **Award 1 mark** for Zeus. | 1 |
| 3 | **Award 1 mark** for gifts for the gods and goddesses. | 1 |
| 4 | **Award 1 mark** for clay. | 1 |
| 5 | **Award 1 mark** for everyday life. | 1 |
| 6 | **Award 1 mark** for Olympia. | 1 |
| 7 | **Award 1 mark** for women. | 1 |
| 8 | **Award 1 mark** for olive wreaths. | 1 |
| 9 | **Award 1 mark** for (large pieces of) cloth. | 1 |
| 10 | **Award 1 mark** for: uncovered | 1 |
| 11 | **Award 1 mark** for pottery/pots/pictures or decorations on pots. | 1 |
| 12 | **Award 1 mark** for Sunday. | 1 |
| 13 | **Award 1 mark** for: warm and welcoming | 1 |
| 14 | **Award 1 mark** for: items | 1 |
| 15 | **Award 1 mark** for: interesting | 1 |
| 16 | **Award 1 mark** for any of the following:<br>● chocolate<br>● delicious<br>● sticky. | 1 |
| 17 | **Award 1 mark** for blue and white. | 1 |
| 18 | **Award 1 mark** for the servant. | 1 |
| 19 | **Award 1 mark** for any of the following:<br>● To keep the servant out.<br>● To keep his daughter in.<br>● To separate them. | 1 |
| 20 | **Award 1 mark** for all correct. | 1 |

| | |
|---|---|
| He banished the servant from the house. | 2 |
| The wealthy man spotted the couple running over the bridge. | 4 |
| The wealthy man had chosen a husband for his daughter. | 1 |
| The beautiful daughter soon died of a broken heart. | 5 |
| The daughter walked up and down the fence. | 3 |

| Q | Answers | Marks |
|---|---------|-------|
| 21 | **Award 2 marks** for two correct reasons.<br>• It was warm and welcoming.<br>• Each room had interesting things from around the world/the house had interesting things in.<br>• Aunty Alice told fascinating stories.<br>• She made delicious cake.<br><br>**Award 1 mark** for one correct reason. | 2 |
| 22 | **a. Award 2 marks** for any three of the following: Africa, Netherlands, Australia, Morocco, India, China.<br>**Award 1 mark** for two correct. | 2 |
| | **b. Award 2 marks** for an answer that says the objects she collected were from her travels.<br>**Award 1 mark** for answers that only mention one specific object such as 'because she had a didgeridoo from Australia'. | 2 |
| 23 | **Award 1 mark** for an answer that explains the moon covers the sun. | 1 |
| 24 | **Award 1 mark** for: park | 1 |
| 25 | **Award 1 mark** for to watch/see the solar eclipse. | 1 |
| 26 | **Award 1 mark** for to protect your eyes. | 1 |
| 27 | **Award 2 marks** for:<br>• Good idea: they protect his/her eyes.<br>• Bad idea: they are ruining his/her style.<br><br>**Award 1 mark** for one of the above. | 2 |
| 28 | **Award 1 mark** for: quickly | 1 |
| 29 | **Award 2 marks** for answers that refer to the sun disappearing/appearing and the people gathering/leaving, such as:<br>• It went dark in the first verse and became light in the final verse.<br>• The crowds gathered in the first verse, and left in the final verse.<br><br>**Award 1 mark** for one of the above. | 2 |
| 30 | **Award 1 mark** for: On the school field | 1 |
| 31 | **Award 1 mark** for afternoon. | 1 |
| 32 | **Award 1 mark** for 200m hurdles. | 1 |
| 33 | **Award 1 mark** for red. | 1 |
| 34 | **Award 1 mark** for a clear reason such as:<br>• She thinks she isn't very good.<br>• She is worried she will fall over.<br>• She thinks everyone will laugh.<br>• She thinks it will be embarrassing. | 1 |

| Q | Answers | Marks |
|---|---------|-------|
| 35 | **Award 2 marks** for embarrassed or upset and for her face went red, she tried to wipe away her tears, she didn't want Amira to see her crying, she was crying.<br><br>**Award 1 mark** for one of the above. | 2 |
| 36 | **Award 3 marks** for any three reasons from the text:<br>● She goes to see if she is all right.<br>● The text says they are best friends.<br>● She puts her arm around her (to comfort her).<br>● She tells her everyone likes her for who she is.<br>● She tells her all the things she is good at.<br>● She cheers her up.<br>● She makes her smile.<br>● She is encouraging.<br>● She smiles at her.<br>● She says, "You can do it!"<br><br>**Award 2 marks** for two correct reasons.<br><br>**Award 1 mark** for one correct reason. | 3 |
| 37 | **Award 1 mark** for: It shows that Jessica was feeling nervous. | 1 |
| 38 | **Award 1 mark** for: It shows how frightened Jessica felt about the hurdles race. | 1 |
| 39 | **Award 1 mark** for all correct. | 1 |

| | |
|---|---|
| Amira told Jessica that her friends and family all liked her for who she was. | 3 |
| The red team celebrated loudly by singing and dancing. | 5 |
| Suddenly, the bell rang and everyone started lining up on the playground. | 2 |
| Jessica ran as fast as she could. | 4 |
| Jessica was crying at lunchtime. | 1 |

| Q | Answers | Marks |
|---|---------|-------|
| 40 | **Award 2 marks** for any feeling that is positive, for example relieved, happy, pleased, proud, excited and for a reason such as the race was over, she didn't come last, she didn't fall over, she did it, her team won, she won a point.<br><br>**Award 1 mark** for one of the above. | 2 |

# Mark scheme for Test C (pages 49–68)

| Q | Answers | Marks |
|---|---------|-------|
| 1 | **Award 1 mark** for: excellent | 1 |
| 2 | **Award 1 mark** for: sugary | 1 |
| 3 | **Award 1 mark** for a net. | 1 |
| 4 | **Award 1 mark** for all three correct:<br>• water<br>• a garden trowel<br>• moist soil or compost | 1 |
| 5 | **Award 2 marks** for any answer that suggests both of the following:<br>• so you don't damage the roots<br>• because the roots are delicate<br>**Award 1 mark** for one of the above. | 2 |
| 6 | **Award 1 mark** for 30cm. | 1 |
| 7 | **Award 1 mark** for June and August. | 1 |
| 8 | **Award 1 mark** for any answer that suggests either of the following:<br>• to stop the plants touching the soil<br>• to stop them rotting. | 1 |
| 9 | **Award 1 mark** for: strawberry cheesecake | 1 |
| 10 | **Award 1 mark** for 150g. | 1 |
| 11 | **Award 1 mark** for answers that suggest: to smear or cover the tin in butter or grease. | 1 |
| 12 | **Award 1 mark** for 2 hours. | 1 |
| 13 | **Award 1 mark** for their/the/our website. | 1 |
| 14 | **Award 1 mark** for: To make them stand out so that the reader notices them. | 1 |
| 15 | **a. Award 1 mark** for: A hanging basket and A pot on the patio.<br>**b. Award 1 mark** for you can grow the plants in pots or hanging baskets. | 1<br>1 |
| 16 | **Award 1 mark** for 38 years. | 1 |
| 17 | **Award 2 marks** for fiery and red. | 2 |
| 18 | **Award 1 mark** for: remained alive | 1 |
| 19 | **Award 1 mark** for six. | 1 |
| 20 | Divorced, beheaded, (died.)<br>Divorced, beheaded, (survived!)<br>**Award 1 mark** for both correct. | 1 |
| 21 | **Award 1 mark** for Arthur. | 1 |
| 22 | **Award 1 mark** for it was against the rules tef the Roman Catholic Church. | 1 |

**SCHOLASTIC** National Curriculum SATs Tests

| Q | Answers | Marks |
|---|---------|-------|
| 23 | **Award 1 mark** for Henry fell in love with her. | 1 |
| 24 | **Award 2 marks** for:<br>• Mary<br>• Elizabeth.<br><br>**Award 1 mark** for one of the above. | 2 |
| 25 | **Award 1 mark** for Edward. | 1 |
| 26 | **Award 1 mark** for any answer that suggests either of the following:<br>• to become king after him<br>• to become heir to the throne. | 1 |
| 27 | **Award 1 mark** for both correct names:<br>• Anne Boleyn<br>• Catherine Howard | 1 |
| 28 | **Award 2 marks** for two reasons from the text, such as:<br>• He thought she was ugly.<br>• She didn't like music and reading.<br>• They didn't like the same things.<br>• They were not a good match.<br><br>**Award 1 mark** for one of the above. | 2 |
| 29 | **Award 1 mark** for: a meadow | 1 |
| 30 | **Award 1 mark** for all lines drawn correctly.<br><br>friendly → Frog<br>old and wise → Tortoise<br>loud and rude → Hare | 1 |
| 31 | **Award 1 mark** for he squashed the flowers (so she couldn't make honey). | 1 |
| 32 | **Award 1 mark** for: To discuss what to do about their new neighbour. | 1 |
| 33 | **Award 1 mark** for any answer that suggests either of the following:<br>• He thought he would win.<br>• Because he was good at running. | 1 |
| 34 | **Award 1 mark** for any word with the same meaning as *spotted*, such as: saw, noticed, spied. | 1 |
| 35 | **Award 1 mark** for: It sounds slow and heavy. | 1 |

| Q | Answers | Marks |
|---|---------|-------|
| 36 | **Award 1 mark** for all correct. | 1 |

| | |
|---|---|
| Hare saw Tortoise slowly step over the finish line. | 5 |
| The day of the race arrived. | 3 |
| One day a new neighbour moved in. | 1 |
| The animals held a meeting. | 2 |
| Hare fell asleep under an oak tree. | 4 |

| Q | Answers | Marks |
|---|---------|-------|
| 37 | **Award 3 marks** for any answer that suggests unhappy, upset, he didn't like it, cross, angry or annoyed and supports it with two pieces of evidence. Such as:<br>• The horrid cold water splashed on him while he was trying to relax.<br>• He couldn't relax anymore.<br>• He went to the meeting with the other animals.<br>• He was bubbling with anger.<br><br>**Award 2 marks** for any answer that suggests unhappy, upset, he didn't like it, cross, angry or annoyed and supports it with one piece of evidence.<br><br>**Award 1 mark** for any answer that suggests unhappy, upset, he didn't like it, cross, angry or annoyed but doesn't support it with evidence. | 3 |
| 38 | **Award 2 marks** for an answer that explains Frog thought he would have to leave the meadow because he thought Tortoise would lose the race/Hare would win.<br><br>**Award 1 mark** for an answer that suggests one of the below:<br>• Frog thought he would have to leave the meadow and find somewhere else to live.<br>• Frog thought Tortoise would lose the race. | 2 |
| 39 | **Award 2 marks** for any answer that suggests a feeling such as sad, upset, disappointed, cross, angry, silly, stupid and supports it with pieces of evidence. Possible responses:<br>• he had fallen asleep.<br>• he would have to move out.<br>• he felt sad because he had lost the race.<br><br>**Award 1 mark** for any answer that suggests unhappy, upset, he didn't like it, cross, angry or annoyed but doesn't support it with evidence. | 2 |
| 40 | **Award 2 marks** for an answer that suggests Hare moved out and provides evidence from the text: 'Whoever is the fastest animal around the meadow gets to stay.'<br><br>**Award 1 mark** for answers that suggest Hare moved out but do not support this with evidence. | 2 |

# QUICK TESTS FOR SATs SUCCESS

## BOOST YOUR CHILD'S CONFIDENCE WITH 10-MINUTE SATs TESTS

- Bite-size mini SATs tests which take just 10 minutes to complete

- Covers key National Test topics

- Full answers and progress chart provided to track improvement

- Available for Years 1 to 6

**Find out more at www.scholastic.co.uk**